DECORATING
BISCUITS

Decorating
BISCUITS

Joanna Farrow

MEREHURST

Contents

Introduction

The art of biscuit decoration has been practised for centuries, dating back to when spicy gingerbreads were gilded with gold paint, studded with whole spices or baked in elaborate moulds to enhance their appearance. In this book, the idea has been developed to cover a wealth of different decorative techniques – some simple and instantly achievable, others rather more intricate and time consuming.

Some of the designs have a distinctly seasonal theme, while others are perfect for more specific occasions such as weddings, christenings and birthdays. Many of the shapes can be used as eyecatching decorations, or even as attractive, personalized gifts. Appealing to adults and children alike, these biscuits are sure to be as much fun to make as they are to receive.

Recipes

Dark gingerbread

410g/13oz/3¼ cups self-raising flour

2 teaspoons ground ginger

½ teaspoon ground cloves

125g/4oz/½ cup firm unsalted butter

125g/4oz/⅔ cup dark muscovado sugar

125g/4oz/⅓ cup black treacle/molasses

1 egg, lightly beaten

makes about 24

preparation time 10 minutes, plus chilling

baking time 12–15 minutes

1 Preheat the oven to 200°C/400°F/Gas Mark 6 and grease two baking/cookie sheets.

2 Put the flour and spices in a food processor. Cut the butter into small pieces, add to the processor and blend until the mixture resembles breadcrumbs. Add the sugar, treacle/molasses and egg, and mix to a dough. Wrap and chill for at least 30 minutes.

3 Roll out the mixture on a floured surface. Cut out rounds or squares and place on the baking sheets. Bake for 12–15 minutes until the shapes have risen slightly and appear a little paler in colour. Leave for 2 minutes, then transfer to a wire rack to cool.

Light gingerbread

350g/12oz/3 cups plain/all-purpose flour

2 teaspoons baking powder

2 teaspoons ground ginger

100g/3½oz/scant ½ cup firm unsalted butter

185g/6oz/1 cup light muscovado sugar

3 tablespoons golden/corn syrup

1 egg, lightly beaten

makes about 24

preparation time 10 minutes, plus chilling time

baking time 12 minutes

1 Preheat the oven to 200°C/400°F/Gas Mark 6 and grease two baking/cookie sheets.

2 Put the flour, baking powder and ginger in a food processor. Cut the butter into small pieces, add to the food processor and blend until the mixture resembles breadcrumbs. Add the sugar, syrup and egg, and blend to a dough. Wrap and chill for at least 30 minutes.

3 Roll out the mixture on a floured surface. Cut out rounds or squares and place on the baking sheets. Bake for about 12 minutes until the shapes turn golden around the edges. Leave for 2 minutes, then transfer to a wire rack to cool.

Vanilla sable

280g/10oz/2¼ cups plain/all-purpose flour
200g/7oz/⅞ cup firm unsalted butter
100g/3½oz/⅘ cup icing/confectioners' sugar
2 egg yolks
1 teaspoon vanilla essence/extract
(For chocolate sable, substitute 30g/1oz/¼ cup cocoa
powder for 30g/1oz/¼ cup of the flour.)

makes about 20
preparation time 10 minutes, plus chilling
baking time 6–10 minutes

1 Preheat the oven to 200°C/400°F/Gas Mark 6 and
grease two baking/cookie sheets.

2 Put the flour in a food processor. Cut the butter into
small pieces, add it to the food processor and blend
together until the mixture resembles breadcrumbs. Add
the sugar, egg yolks and vanilla essence/extract and
blend to a smooth dough. Wrap and chill for an hour.

3 Roll out the mixture on a floured surface, cut out rounds
or squares and place on the baking sheets. Bake for
about 6–10 minutes until the pieces turn golden around
the edges. Transfer the vanilla/chocolate sable shapes to
a wire rack to cool

Icing glaze (single quantity)

1 egg white
1 tablespoon lemon juice
150g/5oz/1¼ cups icing/confectioners' sugar, sifted
preparation time 3 minutes

1 Lightly whisk the egg white and lemon juice in a bowl.

2 Gradually whisk in the icing/confectioners' sugar until
the mixture is smooth and has the consistency of a
pouring cream.

3 Cover the surface of the icing with cling film/plastic
wrap to prevent a crust forming until ready for use.

Royal icing (single quantity)

1 egg white
approx 200g/7oz/1¾ cups icing/confectioners' sugar, sifted
preparation time 3 minutes

1 Lightly whisk the egg white in a bowl. Gradually whisk
in sufficient icing/confectioners' sugar to make a softly
peaking icing.

2 Cover the surface of the icing with cling film/plastic
wrap to prevent a crust forming.

Basic techniques

Working with biscuit/cookie dough

Biscuit/cookie dough is generally easy to work with, even for inexperienced cooks. If you follow a few simple guidelines, biscuits can be made and baked effortlessly, ready for the enjoyment of decorating.

1 Once the biscuit mixture is made, either in the food processor or by hand, it must be chilled for at least 30 minutes – preferably longer – to firm up. Otherwise the mixture can be too soft to work with and will easily lose its shape during baking. For this reason, you may prefer to make it in advance. Store the dough, wrapped in cling film/plastic wrap or foil, for up to two days. It also freezes well for up to 1 month.

2 Cut out the shapes and position the pieces on the baking/cookie sheet. Allow space between each biscuit as the pieces will expand slightly during baking.

3 For larger biscuit shapes, such as the gingerbread cottage on page 90, you may find it easier to cut out the shapes on the baking sheet so they do not distort as you transfer them from the work surface.

4 Rather than waste leftover dough, re-roll and bake the trimmings. They are good for practising decorative techniques and, of course, taste good un-iced!

5 For hanging biscuits, always remember to re-mark the holes after baking because the dough will have expanded slightly on cooking. Do this as soon as the biscuits come out of the oven, while they are still soft.

6 Due to the high sugar content, all biscuits are soft when they first come out of the oven. Therefore, do not be tempted to bake them for extra time – they will quickly turn crisp on cooling. Leave the biscuits on the baking sheets to cool slightly before transferring them to the wire cooling rack, to prevent them from falling apart.

Icing and sugarpaste

Royal icing is easy to make and perfect for piping decorations. Do not make the consistency too stiff, otherwise it will be difficult to squeeze through the small tubes/tips. Incorporate the icing/confectioners' sugar until the icing is softly peaking, rather than stiff.

Cake decorating supply shops stock a wide range of sugarpaste/rolled fondant colours while supermarkets usually only sell a few basic ones. If you just need a small quantity of several colours, buy a small pack of white sugarpaste and knead in the appropriate colours. Generally, paste colours give the richest tones while liquid ones make more pastel shades.

All icings can be prepared a day in advance and stored in a cool place or in the refrigerator. For royal icing and icing glaze, cover the actual surface with clear film, and keep sugarpaste tightly wrapped in cling film/plastic wrap or foil to prevent a crust forming.

Making a paper piping bag

Paper piping bags are particularly useful for decorating as the tip can be snipped off, thus removing the need for a tube/tip. (However, tubes are useful for piping intricate shapes because a snipped paper tip does not always pipe perfect lines.) Paper bags are also disposable of course, hence no cleaning out and washing up!

1 Cut a 19cm/7½in square of greaseproof paper/baking parchment in half diagonally.

2 Holding one triangle with the longest side away from you, curl the left hand point over to meet the point nearest you, shaping a cone.

3 Curl the right hand point over the cone, bringing the points neatly together. Then fold the points over several times to secure the bag in place.

Fan-assisted ovens

Remember that fan-assisted ovens should be set at lower temperatures than conventional ovens – a general rule is 20°C cooler than the Celsius temperature stated.

Using templates

Many of the biscuit designs require one or more of the templates on pages 124–126. Greaseproof paper/baking parchment can be used although a plain sheet of paper tends to be easier to work with. Rest the template on the rolled out dough and cut carefully around it. For basic shapes, a small sharp knife is usually adequate. For more intricate shapes, a scalpel tends to be easier to manage.

Melting chocolate

Melted plain, milk or white chocolate can be used for coating biscuits or for piping decorations.

1 Break the chocolate into small, even-sized pieces and put it in a heatproof bowl.

2 Place the bowl over a small pan of very gently simmering water and leave the chocolate to melt. Make sure the base of the bowl does not touch the water or the chocolate will overheat.

3 Stir gently to check that no lumps remain before use.

TIP Chocolate can also be melted in the microwave. Break up the chocolate into a bowl and allow 1½–2 minutes for 90g/3oz chocolate. Leave to stand for a minute then stir gently. Microwave again if lumps remain.

Springtime

Flower garlands

Unlike most doughs, this mixture is piped rather than rolled out. It does require patience to pipe the garlands – but the results are well worth the effort.

1 Preheat the oven to 180°C/350°F/Gas Mark 4 and grease the two baking/cookie sheets. Mix together the butter and caster/superfine sugar, to form a very pale, creamy paste. Add the flour and lemon juice and stir to a smooth mixture. Transfer the paste to a piping bag fitted with a large star writing tube/tip. (You might find it easier to add only half the mixture, and top the bag up with more mixture as you work.)

2 Pipe rings of small scallops on to the baking sheets so that each one just touches the next. Twist the end of the

185g/6½oz/¾ cup unsalted butter, softened
55g/2oz/¼ cup caster/superfine sugar
250g/8oz/2 cups plain/all-purpose flour
4 teaspoons lemon juice
icing and decoration
55g/2oz/¼ cup caster sugar
small amount of lightly beaten egg white
several miniature roses
12 white or coloured sugared almonds
150g/5oz/1¼ cups icing/confectioners' sugar, sifted
6–8 teaspoons lemon juice or rosewater

equipment
2 baking/cookie sheets
large nylon piping bag
1cm/½in star writing tube/tip
wire cooling rack
polythene bag
paintbrush
rolling pin
makes 12
baking time 12 minutes

bag firmly after piping each shape. Bake the garlands for about 12 minutes until they turn a pale, golden colour. Leave the garlands to stand on the baking sheets for 2 minutes to harden and cool slightly, before transferring them to a wire cooling rack.

3 To make the sugared rose petals, put the caster/superfine sugar and egg white in separate small containers. Remove the petals from one of the miniature roses. Coat both sides of one of the rose petals with a small amount of egg white. (Use a paintbrush for coating the petal, or simply rub the surface with your thumb and forefinger dipped in the egg white.)

4 Sprinkle the petal surfaces with caster sugar and place them on a sheet of paper to dry. Repeat this process for the other petals – you will need about five petals for each of the garlands.

5 Put the sugared almonds in a polythene bag and lightly beat them with the end of a rolling pin to break the nuts into small pieces.

6 Stir together the icing/confectioners' sugar and lemon juice or rosewater, to create a smooth mixture. Use the small teaspoon to drizzle a small amount of icing over each garland.

7 While the icing is still soft, arrange some of the sugared rose petals over each garland. Gently press them into the icing. Arrange the broken pieces of sugared almonds between the petals. Put the garlands aside to set for 1–2 hours. Then store the shapes in an airtight container for up to two days, stacking them no more than two deep. Interleave layers of greaseproof paper/baking parchment between the garlands, to help prevent them from sticking.

TIPS Make sure the butter you use is really soft before creaming it with the sugar, otherwise it will be very difficult to pipe from the bag. It is best to leave the butter at room temperature for several hours or microwave it briefly.

Once sugared, the flower petals should keep for several weeks in a cool, dry place, enabling you to make them well in advance.

Miniature roses are just the right size for decorating biscuits but you could use any other small edible flowers that are to hand. Tiny primroses and violets are all particularly effective, and small herb flowers are an unusual, attractive variation.

If you are very short of preparation time, you could always buy tiny crystallized roses or violets from a delicatessen or cake decorating supplier.

Valentine hearts

These pretty, piped hearts, with their different designs, make ideal gifts or decorations for Valentine, engagement, wedding or anniversary celebrations.

1 Preheat the oven to 200°C/400°F/Gas Mark 6 and grease the two baking/cookie sheets. Roll out the vanilla sable mixture on a floured surface and use the large cutter to cut out the hearts. Transfer them to the baking sheet and bake for 8 minutes or until they turn golden around the edges. Leave on the baking sheets for 2 minutes, then transfer them to a wire rack to cool.

2 Using a palette knife/metal spatula, spread the icing glaze over the hearts. Try to achieve a thin, even layer, spreading the icing just to the edges of the shapes.

vanilla sable mixture (see page 9)
icing and decoration
icing glaze (see page 9)
50g/1¾oz sugarpaste/rolled fondant
icing/confectioners' sugar for dusting
royal icing (see page 9)
silver dragees
equipment
2 baking/cookie sheets
rolling pin
7.5cm/3in and 1.25cm/½in heart-shaped cutters

wire cooling rack
palette knife/metal spatula
paper piping bag
medium writing tube/tip
makes 16–18
baking time 8 minutes

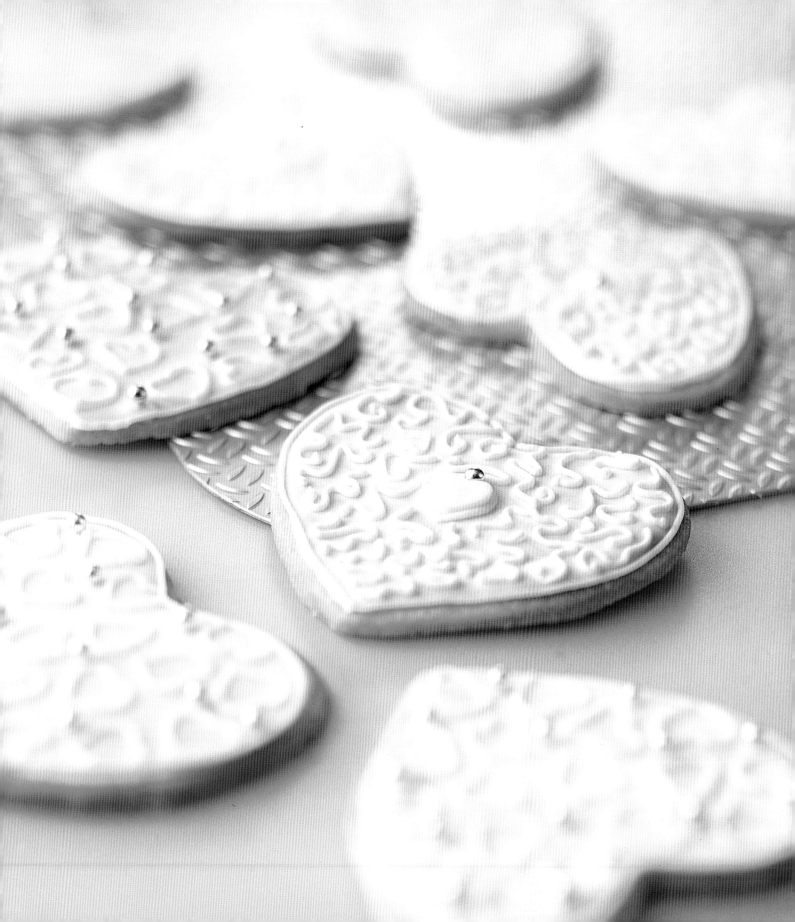

3 Thinly roll the sugarpaste/rolled fondant on a surface dusted with icing/confectioners' sugar. Cut out heart shapes from the sugarpaste, using the small cutter.

4 Put the royal icing in a piping bag fitted with a medium writing tube/tip. Pipe a small amount of icing in the centre of about half of the biscuits. Position the sugarpaste hearts over the icing and secure them in place. Leave aside for about 30 minutes until touch dry.

5 Use the small cutter to impress heart shapes into the icing on the remaining biscuits. Leave about 5mm/¼in between each heart and adjust the angles of each.

6 Pipe a line around the edge of each biscuit, then pipe lines around the edges of the single heart biscuits and secure a dragee at the top of each. Pipe decorative wavy filigree lines all over the glaze.

7 Pipe over the impressed lines on the remaining biscuits to accentuate the heart shapes and secure dragees at intervals between the hearts, securing each with a dot of icing from the bag.

TIP For added decoration, make holes near the tops of the hearts before baking so that they can be threaded with ribbons, which can then be tied in bows.

Mother's day flowers

A plain, round biscuit cutter is all you need to shape these simple flower biscuits, unless, of course, you have a similarly-shaped flower cutter.

1 Preheat the oven to 200°C/400°F/Gas Mark 6. Grease two baking/cookie sheets. Roll out the sable mixture on a floured surface and cut into 2.5cm/1in wide strips.

2 Using the cutter, cut out semi-circular shapes from the strips, then cut out the straight side from each semi-circle to make petal shapes (see overleaf).

3 Arrange a petal on the baking sheet and brush the tip with a little lightly beaten egg white. Position another petal over the top and press down gently to secure. Arrange

vanilla sable mixture (see page 9)
small amount of lightly beaten egg white
icing and decoration
100g/3½oz/scant ½ cup unsalted butter, softened
210g/7oz/1¾ cups icing/confectioners' sugar, sifted
green and yellow food colourings
equipment
2 baking/cookie sheets
7.5cm/3in round biscuit/cookie cutter
wire cooling rack
paper piping bags

small star tube/tip
makes 16–18
baking time 8 minutes

three more petals to assemble a complete flower, brushing the end of each with egg white. Assemble the remaining flowers in the same way. Re-roll the trimmings to make more flowers.

4 Bake for about 8 minutes until they turn a pale, golden colour around the edges. Leave on the baking sheets for 5 minutes, then transfer to a wire rack to cool.

5 To make the buttercream, beat the butter in a bowl until soft. Add the icing/confectioners' sugar and beat well until pale and creamy, adding a few drops of boiling water if necessary to make creaming easier.

6 Spoon a quarter of the mixture into a piping bag and snip off the tip. Spoon another quarter into a bowl and colour it pale green. Feed this into another piping bag and snip off the tip. Colour the remaining buttercream pale yellow and feed into a bag fitted with a star tube/tip.

7 Use the yellow buttercream to pipe around the edges of the petals, keeping clear of the centres of the flowers.

8 Use the buttercream in the other two piping bags to pipe dots into the centres of the flowers. Leave aside to firm up before storing the shapes in a container layered with greaseproof paper/baking parchment.

Chocolate checkerboard

These buttery, two-tone squares are easy to shape and the contrast is extremely effective. The melted chocolate adds a perfect finishing touch.

1 Preheat the oven to 200°C/400°F/Gas Mark 6 and lightly grease the large baking/cookie sheet. On a floured surface, roll out the vanilla sable mixture to a 30cm x 12cm/12in x 4½in rectangle, about 1.5cm/⅝in thick. Keep the dough in a neat block as you work, so that very little of the mixture will need to be trimmed off once the checkerboard pattern is shaped. Repeat with the chocolate mixture.

2 Brush the vanilla dough with a small amount of beaten egg white. This will help the two pastes to adhere

vanilla sable mixture (see page 9)
chocolate sable mixture (see page 9)
small amount of beaten egg white
small amount of flour
icing and decoration
75g/2½oz plain/semi-sweet chocolate
75g/2½oz white chocolate
equipment
large baking/cookie sheet
rolling pin
pastry brush

sharp knife
wire cooling rack
paper piping bags
makes 60
baking time 12–15 minutes

together. Carefully lay the chocolate dough over the top of the vanilla dough.

Use a sharp, lightly floured knife to cut the mixture in half, lengthways. Brush one of the halves with egg white and then stack the other half on top, so that the colours alternate. Take care to line up the cut edges of the doughs. Carefully trim off the uncut edges of the dough.

Use the lightly floured knife to cut the dough block lengthways into four even-sized strips. Re-flour the knife after each cut if the dough begins to stick to the surface of the blade.

Re-assemble the stack so that the colours alternate, creating a checkerboard design. Do not forget to brush each layer with egg white to secure them together.

Slice the stack widthways into 5mm/¼in slices and transfer the pieces to the baking sheet, spacing them slightly apart from each other. Bake for 12–15 minutes until the squares just begin to darken around the edges. Leave the pieces on the baking sheet for 2 minutes before transferring them to a wire cooling rack.

Break the plain and white chocolate into pieces in separate bowls, and melt them over a saucepan of hot

water. Put the melted chocolates in paper piping bags and snip off the merest tip of each. Use the plain chocolate to pipe decorative dots and lines on to half the biscuits. Use the white chocolate to pipe decorations over the remaining squares.

Leave the squares to set in a cool place for about 2 hours before transferring them to an airtight container.

TIPS Shaping these checkerboards is so much easier, and the definition of the pattern will be clearly distinguishable, if the dough is really well chilled. If the mixture starts sticking to the knife, particularly when you come to step 5, put the dough in the freezer for about 10 minutes to firm up. Likewise, if the dough is soft once the biscuits have been shaped, pop them in the freezer on the baking sheets for a little while and they will retain a better shape while baking.

If you prefer a generous amount of chocolate on your biscuits, melt some extra chocolate and dip the backs of the squares into the liquid. Allow the excess chocolate to drip back into the pan, before placing the biscuits, chocolate-side down, on greaseproof paper/baking parchment. Alternatively, dip just the sides of the squares in chocolate, and then roll them in chopped hazelnuts.

Chocolate mosaic eggs

Ideal for chocoholics, these eggs use three kinds of chocolate. For presentation, try hanging them from window frames, or put them in a box lined with tissue paper.

1 Preheat the oven to 180°C/350°F/Gas Mark 4 and grease two large baking/cookie sheets. Put the flour, spice and butter in a food processor and blend until the mixture resembles fine breadcrumbs. Add the apricots, sugar and egg, and mix thoroughly to create a dough. (If you do not have a food processor, you can mix the flour and spice in a bowl, and then rub the butter into this by hand. Then mix in the apricots, sugar and egg.)

2 Turn the dough mixture out on to a lightly floured surface and roll it out to 0.5cm/¼in thickness. Use the

225g/8oz/2 cups plain/all-purpose flour
2 teaspoons ground mixed spice
125g/4oz/½ cup unsalted butter
125g/4oz/¾ cup dried apricots, roughly chopped
150g/5oz/¾ cup light muscovado sugar
1 egg
icing and decoration
100g/3½oz milk chocolate
100g/3½oz plain/semi-sweet chocolate
100g/3½oz white chocolate
fine ribbon

equipment
2 large baking/cookie sheets
rolling pin
6cm/2½in round biscuit/cookie cutter
metal skewer
wire cooling rack
paper piping bags
makes 24
baking time 12–15 minutes

cutter to cut out as many round shapes as possible. Odd scraps of dough can be pushed together and re-rolled, to ensure that all the mixture gets used – you should be able to make about 24 pieces.

To make the circles into egg shapes, place about three pieces in a row and push a rolling pin over them, increasing the pressure as you roll. The circles should become elongated and egg-shaped.

Transfer the pieces to the baking sheets. Use the metal skewer to make holes in the top ends of the shapes about 1cm/½in away from the edges. Bake for 12–15 minutes

until golden. Re-mark the holes if the biscuits have risen slightly during cooking. Transfer the pieces to a wire rack and leave to cool.

Break up the chocolate into separate bowls and melt each over a saucepan of hot water. Put the milk chocolate in a piping bag and snip off the merest tip. Pipe a line on to each egg shape, about 3mm/⅛in from the edge. Pipe further random lines inside the piped border, first in one direction and then the other.

Put the plain/semi-sweet chocolate into another piping bag and snip off the tip. Use this to fill in some of the

patterned shapes created by the milk chocolate piping. Aim to fill around half the number of shapes.

7 Use the metal skewer to ease the melted chocolate into the corners of the piped shapes. (Tapping the biscuit gently on the surface sometimes helps to spread the chocolate.) Do not be tempted to over-fill the areas – otherwise the chocolate may run over the edges.

8 Put the white chocolate into another piping bag and use this to fill the remaining sections of the biscuits. Again, use the (cleaned) skewer to take the chocolate right up to the edges. Leave to set slightly. Pipe more milk chocolate

over the original lines to accentuate the shapes. Leave the eggs aside to set in a cool place before storing on a tray, covered with cling film/plastic wrap for up to two days.

9 Cut varying lengths of ribbon and thread these through the holes in the biscuits so that they can be hung up.

TIP Cut the smallest amount possible off the tip of the milk chocolate piping bag. This is because warm chocolate flows out very quickly, and so you need to be able to control the icing. (You can easily cut off a fraction more if necessary.) The recipe works equally well with the vanilla or chocolate sable mixture on page 9.

Easter chicks

These cute chicks make bright, fun gifts or ideal table decorations at birthday and Christening parties. Tie them in bundles or arrange them in a nest display.

1 Preheat the oven to 200°C/400°F/Gas Mark 6 and grease two baking/cookie sheets. Trace the two chick templates (see page 124) on to paper and cut them out. Roll out the chosen dough on a floured surface and cut out the chick shapes using the templates and a sharp knife or scalpel. Transfer the pieces to the baking sheets.

2 If you are using the vanilla sable mixture, bake the chicks for about 8–10 minutes. If you are using the light gingerbread mixture, bake the chicks for about 12 minutes. Leave the chicks to stand on the baking

vanilla sable or light gingerbread mixture (see pages 8 and 9)

icing and decoration
yellow and blue food colourings
icing glaze (see page 9)
royal icing (see page 9)
30g/1oz orange sugarpaste/rolled fondant icing/confectioners' sugar, for dusting

equipment
2 baking/cookie sheets
paper for template (see page 124)
rolling pin
sharp knife or scalpel
wire cooling rack
pastry brush
paper piping bag
medium writing tube/tip
fine paintbrush
makes about 16
baking time 8–12 minutes

sheets for 2 minutes, before transferring them to a wire rack to cool.

3 Add some yellow food colouring to the icing glaze. Then, using a pastry brush, spread a layer of glaze over all the chicks. Take the glaze right up to the edges to create a thin, even surface.

4 Spoon some royal icing into a piping bag fitted with a medium writing tube/tip. Carefully pipe around the outlines of the wings, then around the edges of the chicks. Next, pipe blobs of icing for the eyes. Leave them to dry for about an hour.

5 Thinly roll the orange sugarpaste/rolled fondant over a surface dusted with icing/confectioners' sugar and cut out shapes for the beaks. For the chicks in profile, cut a beak shape using the template as a size guide. For the other chicks, cut out tiny diamond shapes, then pinch them gently to fold the paste into beak shapes. Secure the beaks to the chicks with a dampened paintbrush. Dilute a small amount of blue food colouring with water and use this to paint in the centres of the eyes.

TIP For a special presentation, arrange the chicks in small boxes, baskets or other containers and surround them with shredded paper and chocolate mini eggs.

Chocolate box

A chocolate lover's heaven! These lavishly coated chocolate goodies are great for serving with coffee, or as a boxed-up gift at any time of year.

1 Finely chop the butter and put this, along with the flour and cocoa powder, into a food processor. Blend until the mixture resembles fine breadcrumbs. Mix in the sugar, egg yolks and black treacle/molasses to form a dough.

2 Roll the mixture under the palms of your hands into a thick, even sausage, about 30cm/12in long and 4cm/1½in wide. Neaten the ends of the sausage, then wrap in cling film/plastic wrap and chill for at least 30 minutes. Preheat the oven to 200°C/400°F/Gas Mark 6 and grease a large baking/cookie sheet.

60g/2oz/¼ cup butter
175g/6oz/1½ cups self-raising flour
25g/1oz/¼ cup cocoa powder
60g/2oz/⅓ cup light muscovado sugar
2 egg yolks
60g/2oz/⅙ cup black treacle/molasses

icing and decoration
150g/5oz white chocolate
150g/5oz milk chocolate
150g/5oz plain/semi-sweet chocolate
10–12 chocolate-coated coffee beans

cocoa powder for dusting

equipment
cling film/plastic wrap
large baking/cookie sheet
sharp knife
wire cooling rack
greaseproof paper/baking parchment
grater
paper piping bags

makes about 30

baking time 10 minutes

3 Use a sharp knife to cut the mixture into 8mm/³⁄₈in thick slices and transfer them to the baking sheet. Bake for 10 minutes until slightly risen, then transfer the pieces to a wire rack to cool.

4 Finely grate 15g/¹⁄₂oz white chocolate. Melt the remaining white chocolate, and the milk and plain/semi-sweet chocolates in separate bowls. Line a tray with greaseproof paper/baking parchment.

5 Dip a third of the biscuits in the melted white chocolate, allowing excess chocolate to drip into the bowl. Transfer to the tray and sprinkle with grated white chocolate.

6 Place a spoonful of melted milk and plain chocolate into separate piping bags and keep in a warm place. Coat half the biscuits in the remaining milk chocolate and half in the plain chocolate, using a fork as before, and transfer them to the paper-lined tray.

7 Snip the merest tip off the two piping bags. Scribble freehand lines of milk chocolate over each of the plain chocolate-covered biscuits.

8 Pipe swirls of plain chocolate over the milk chocolate-covered biscuits and decorate with a chocolate coffee bean. Leave the tray of biscuits in a cool place to set.

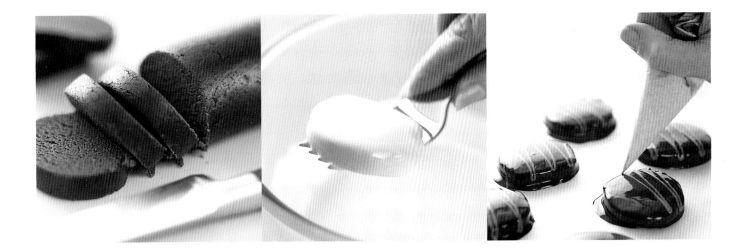

Special occasions

Butterflies

Use contrasting colours, such as those shown here, to decorate these butterflies. Once set, arrange them in a tissue-lined shallow box to make a stunning gift.

1 Preheat the oven to 200°C/400°F/Gas Mark 6 and grease two baking/cookie sheets. Trace the butterfly templates on page 125 on to paper and cut them out. Roll out the vanilla sable mixture on a floured surface and cut out the butterfly shapes using the templates and a sharp knife or scalpel.

2 Transfer the shapes to the baking sheets and re-roll the trimmings to make more shapes. Bake the butterflies for about 8 minutes until they turn a pale golden colour around the edges. Leave the pieces on the baking sheets

vanilla sable mixture (see page 9)

icing and decoration

double quantity of royal icing (see page 9)

blue or purple and green or lilac food colourings

small white cake decorating stamens

equipment

2 baking/cookie sheets

paper for template (see page 125)

rolling pin

sharp knife or scalpel

wire cooling rack

paper piping bags

fine writing tube/tip

cocktail sticks/toothpicks

makes 20–24

baking time 8 minutes

for 5 minutes before transferring them to a wire rack so that they can cool.

Fit a paper piping bag with a fine writing tube/tip. Fill the bag with a small amount of the royal icing. Spoon some more royal icing into another piping bag.

Divide the remaining icing between two bowls. Colour the icing in one bowl blue or purple, and the icing in the other bowl green or lilac. Thin each amount of icing with a few drops of water. A flat surface should form when the icing is left to stand for a minute. Transfer the coloured icings to piping bags.

Using the royal icing in the bag fitted with the writing tube/tip, pipe a line of icing around the edges of the front wings, then around the back wings so the ends almost meet in the centre.

Snip off the tip of the piping bag with the remaining white icing so the icing flows in a thick line. Use this to pipe a coil shape down the centres of the butterflies, allowing the icing to trail off to a point at the end.

Snip off the tip of the piping bag containing the blue or purple icing. Using a scribbling action, flood the wing sections of one butterfly with icing to create a lacy effect.

(If you overfill the sections with icing, it will spread to fill the wings entirely. This also looks effective although you will not achieve the lacy texture.) Ease the icing into the wing tip areas with cocktail sticks/toothpicks.

8 Snip off the tip of the piping bag containing the green or lilac icing. Pipe three small dots on to the back wings of the iced biscuit.

9 Pipe three larger dots of icing into the icing on the front wings. Push a cocktail stick into each dot of icing and draw it down the length of the wing to create a feathered finish. Complete about half the number of butterflies in this way, then reverse the colours to decorate the remaining butterfly shapes.

10 Pipe a large dot of white icing at the front of each body. Cut the stamens down to 1cm/½in lengths and press two into each butterfly for antennae. Leave to set until the icing is hard. Store in a large, airtight tin, interleaved with greaseproof paper/baking parchment.

TIP Remember to complete each butterfly with coloured icing before going on to the next shape. This is because the icing forms a crust quite quickly and delays could prevent the colours from feathering together properly.

Christening biscuits

An assortment of prettily decorated biscuits makes an eye-catching spread of pastel colours for a Christening celebration or little girl's party.

1 Preheat the oven to 200°C/400°F/Gas Mark 6 and lightly grease two baking/cookie sheets. Thinly roll out the vanilla sable mixture on a floured surface and cut out shapes using the cutters. Re-roll the trimmings to make more biscuits. (If you do not have many types of cutters, use a knife to cut out 5cm/2in squares. Alternatively, make diamond shapes by cutting the dough into thick strips and then cutting diagonal lines across the strips.)

2 Place the shapes on the baking sheets and bake for around 6–8 minutes, until the pieces turn a pale, golden

vanilla sable mixture (see page 9)
icing and decoration
double quantity royal icing (see page 9)
pink, blue and yellow food colourings
silver dragees
equipment
2 baking/cookie sheets
selection of small biscuit/cookie cutters, about 5cm/2in in diameter; such as heart, petal, diamond, star, circle and teardrop
wire cooling rack

paper piping bags
makes 60
baking time 6–8 minutes

colour around the edges. Leave to stand for a couple of minutes, before transferring to a wire rack to cool.

Divide the royal icing equally into four bowls. Add a little pink colouring to one bowl, blue to the second and yellow to the third. The remaining portion of royal icing should be left white. Transfer the coloured icings to separate piping bags and snip off the tip of each so the icing flows in a fine line.

Thin the white icing with a few drops of water to give it a slightly thinner consistency than the coloured varieties. Spoon this mixture into another piping bag and snip off a

slightly larger tip so that the icing flows in a line about 5mm/¼in thick.

To decorate the stars and diamond-shaped biscuits, pipe three alternate lines of blue and yellow icing around the edges of the biscuits, leaving a small gap between each line. Fill in the centres of the shapes with dots of icing in both colours.

To decorate the heart and petal shapes, pipe large dots of pink or yellow icing around the edges of the biscuits. Pipe an additional row of pink or yellow dots inside the first line. Press silver dragees at evenly spaced intervals

into the icing. Work on a couple of biscuits at a time, so that the icing is still soft enough to secure the dragees.

7 To decorate the round biscuits, pipe swirls of the white icing over the biscuits. Work from the edges into the centre, letting the icing flood over the surface a little. Use the same technique for the teardrop shapes, bringing the icing to a point. Pipe casual lines of blue and pink icing over the white, so that the colours run into each other slightly.

8 Leave the shapes aside for about 2 hours. Once completely set, arrange the pieces in shallow, airtight containers, stacking them no more than two deep. Weave sheets of greaseproof paper/baking parchment between each layer to help protect the shapes and prevent the icing from melting, or becoming crushed.

TIPS These shapes would also make a good choice for a wedding celebration. Use simple white icing or match the colour scheme of the dresses and flowers.

Made using Christmas cutters and vibrant icing colours, the small biscuits would also make ideal decorations for the festive season. Use small cutters such as holly leaves, stars and angel shapes for a seasonal feel.

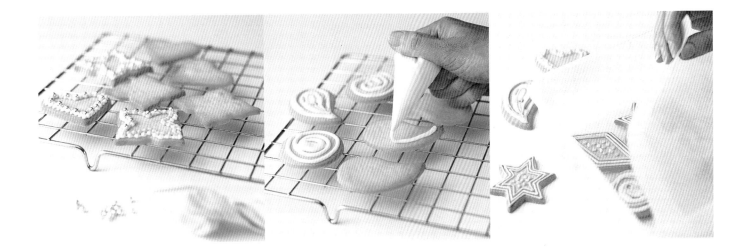

Birthday initials

These little apricot shortbreads can be decorated with the initials of guests at a birthday party, or with a special celebratory message.

1 Preheat the oven to 200°C/400°F/Gas Mark 6. Grease the baking tin/pan and line it with greaseproof paper/baking parchment. Then grease the paper. Reserve a third of the vanilla sable mixture, and roll out the remainder into a rectangle about the size of the tin/pan base. Place the mixture in the tin, pressing it around the corners to form an even layer. Prick the base with a fork.

2 Bake for 20 minutes until just beginning to colour around the edges. Meanwhile, press the jam through the sieve into a bowl using the back of a spoon. Add a few

vanilla sable mixture (see page 9)

icing and decoration

250g/8oz apricot jam

small amount of orange food colouring (optional)

royal icing (see page 9)

silver or gold dragees

equipment

28cm x 18cm/11in x 7in rectangular, shallow baking tin/pan

greaseproof paper/baking parchment

rolling pin

sieve

small alphabet cutters

sharp knife

paper piping bag

medium writing tube/tip

makes 18

baking time 35 minutes

drops of orange food colouring if you wish. Spread the jam in an even layer over the baked mixture in the tin.

Roll out the remaining dough on a floured surface into a long strip. Cut out two 28cm x 1cm/11in x ½in strips and place them over the jam, against the long sides of the tin. Cut two 18cm x 1cm/7in x ½in strips and position them along the short sides. Cut two 28cm x 2cm/11in x ¾in strips and arrange them at even spaces down the length of the tin. Finally, cut five 18cm x 2cm/7in x ¾in strips and position them at even intervals across the width of the tin. The aim is to create a lattice effect across the surface of the base biscuit.

Re-roll the trimmings and cut out the letters using the alphabet cutters or a knife. Arrange these in the individual squares. Bake for a further 15 minutes or until just beginning to colour. Leave to cool in the tin.

Lift the biscuit out of the tin and peel away the lining paper. Trim off the edges of the biscuit, then cut through the strips carefully to make individual squares.

Put some royal icing in a piping bag and pipe lines around the edges of each square, pressing a dragee into each corner as you work. Pipe further lines over the letters. Leave aside to set and store for up to four days.

Festive parcels

Decorated with almonds and exotic dried fruits, shortbreads can be enjoyed on any occasion. Bunched into parcels with ribbon, they make stylish decorations.

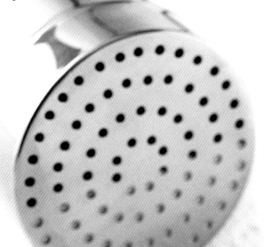

185g/6oz/1½ cups plain/all-purpose flour
125g/4oz/½ cup unsalted butter
60g/2oz/¼ cup caster/superfine sugar
icing and decoration
150g/5oz/1 cup mixed dried fruits such as
mango or papaya
25g/1oz/¼ cup slivered almonds
100g/3½oz/¾ cup icing/
confectioners' sugar
4–5 teaspoons rosewater
length of wired ribbon

1 Preheat the oven to 170°C/325°F/Gas Mark 3. Grease the baking tin/pan, line it with the greaseproof paper/baking parchment, and then grease the paper. Cut the butter into small pieces and put this, along with the flour, into a food processor. Keep the machine turned on until the mixture resembles fine breadcrumbs. Add the sugar and blend until the mixture forms a paste. (Alternatively, put the flour in a bowl and add the finely chopped butter. Rub the butter into the flour with your fingertips, until the mixture begins to bind together. Then add the sugar and mix to the paste in the same way.)

equipment
28cm x 18cm/11in x 7in rectangular, shallow baking tin/pan
greaseproof paper/baking parchment
sharp knife
wire cooling rack
makes 10 parcels
baking time 35 minutes

2 Pack the paste into the tin and press it down with your fingertips, to create a level surface. Prick the base with a fork and bake the mixture for about 35 minutes, until it turns a slight golden colour around the edges.

3 Meanwhile, cut the dried pieces of fruit into very small pieces. Lightly toast the almonds. Add the icing/confectioners' sugar to the rosewater and beat the mixture together until it forms the consistency of a thin, pouring cream.

4 While still warm, make deep cuts into the mixture with a knife. The idea is to create small 'fingers', each measuring about 9cm x 1.5cm/3½ x ⅝in. Leave aside to cool for about 10 minutes.

5 Spread the icing over the baked mixture, until it is covered with a thin, even layer. Make sure that you can still see the cut lines through the icing. (You may not need all the icing.)

6 Decorate each shortbread finger with a row of dried fruits and nuts, then leave them to cool completely.

7 Using a large, sharp knife, trace the cut marks and separate into fingers. Tie into bundles with the ribbon.

Seashore shapes

Making two or three different biscuits with the same theme allows the designs to complement each other. These seaside shapes are ideal for summer occasions.

1 Preheat the oven to 200°C/400°F/Gas Mark 6. Grease two baking/cookie sheets. Trace the shell and starfish templates on page 124 on to paper and cut them out. Roll out the gingerbread mixture on a floured surface and cut out the shell and starfish shapes using the templates and a sharp knife or scalpel. (Make about the same amount of each shape.) Transfer the shapes to the prepared baking sheets and re-roll the trimmings to make more shapes.

2 Bake for about 12 minutes until the shapes begin to darken around the edges. Leave them on the baking

light gingerbread mixture (see page 8)

icing and decoration
175g/6oz/¾ cup unsalted butter, softened
350g/12oz/3 cups icing/confectioners' sugar, sifted
1 tablespoon cocoa powder, sifted
pink food colouring

equipment
2 baking/cookie sheets
paper for template (see page 124)
rolling pin
sharp knife or scalpel
wire cooling rack
paper piping bags
makes 34–38
baking time 12 minutes

sheets for about 2 minutes to harden, before transferring them to a wire rack to cool.

3 To make the buttercream, beat the butter in a bowl until soft and creamy. Gradually beat in the icing/confectioners' sugar until the mixture is smooth and pale. (If the mixture remains firm, add a few drops of boiling water to soften it.) Transfer a large spoonful of the buttercream to a separate bowl and beat in the cocoa powder to make chocolate buttercream. Place in a paper piping bag and snip off the tip. Transfer about a third of the remaining buttercream to a separate bowl and beat in a little pink food colouring. Transfer to another piping bag and snip

off the tip. Place some of the plain buttercream in a third piping bag and snip off the tip.

4 Pipe a line of buttercream around the edges of the starfish, about 3mm/⅛in away from the edges. Pipe two or three more lines just inside the first. (Do not worry about making the piping too perfect on the biscuits. The 'casual' look of the piping is effective on these shapes and is particularly appropriate to buttercream.)

5 On the scallop shapes, fill in the square ends with buttercream, then pipe looped lines of buttercream up to the scalloped edges and back to the base.

6 On the winkle shapes, pipe semi-circles of icing on to each section of the shells, starting at the pointed end. Fill in the biscuits with lines of piping, running lengthways across the surface.

7 Fill in the centres of the starfish biscuits with several lines of pink buttercream. Decorate the centres of the starfish with dots of the chocolate buttercream.

8 Use the chocolate and pink buttercream to pipe decorative details on to the other shapes. Store the biscuits in a single layer in a cool place for up to two days until ready to serve.

TIPS Young children tend to love these kinds of shapes, although you may prefer to use brighter colours as decoration for birthday parties.

Do not stack the shapes during storage as buttercream never sets hard and the icing may become damaged.

This recipe produces a large quantity of biscuit mixture, so you may prefer to use only half the amount and freeze the remaining dough for a later date. Alternatively, you could simply make plain gingerbread biscuits – the buttercream quantity can easily be halved, to ensure there is no wastage.

Feathered tuiles

The piped decoration on these stylish tuiles is completed before they are even baked, so all you have to do is shape them once they come out of the oven.

1 Preheat the oven to 190°C/375°F/Gas Mark 5. Line two baking/cookie sheets with bakewell/non-stick paper and lightly grease the paper. Melt the butter.

2 Whisk the egg whites in a bowl with the sugar until smooth. Whisk in the flour, cream and melted butter to make a loose paste. Spoon 3 tablespoons of the mixture into a small bowl and beat in the cocoa powder until smooth. Transfer the cocoa paste to the piping bag and snip off the tip so that the paste flows in a line about 3mm/$\frac{1}{8}$in thick.

30g/1oz/2 tablespoons unsalted butter

3 egg whites

100g/3$\frac{1}{2}$oz/$\frac{1}{2}$ cup caster/superfine sugar

5 tablespoons plain/all-purpose flour

2 tablespoons double/heavy cream

2 teaspoons cocoa powder, sifted

equipment

2 baking/cookie sheets

bakewell/non-stick paper

paper piping bag

rolling pin

wire cooling rack

makes 20

baking time 8 minutes

3 Place 6 scant tablespoons of the paste on to one baking sheet. Spread each to about 7cm/2¾in in diameter, and allow plenty of space between each.

4 Pipe a small amount of the chocolate paste into each circle of mixture. You can make a variety of patterns, including wavy lines, coils or dots. However, do keep the piping about 1cm/½in away from the edge of each piece, to prevent it bleeding away.

5 Bake in the oven for about 8 minutes until the edges are golden. (Prepare a second batch of tuiles while the first are baking.)

6 Once baked, peel the paper off the tuiles and lay them over a rolling pin so that they set with a curved shape. When the second batch are baked, the first can be transferred from the rolling pin to a wire rack.

TIPS If the baked biscuits turn crisp before you have managed to shape them around the rolling pin, pop them back in the oven for a few moments. This will help to soften them.

For extra decoration, roll the edges in 75g/3oz plain/semi-sweet melted chocolate. Then place them on a sheet of greaseproof paper/baking parchment to set.

Wedding place names

Small, rectangular vanilla biscuits make excellent 'place names' for wedding tables. If you have a colour scheme, you can always add highlights to the icing.

1 Preheat the oven to 200°C/400°F/Gas Mark 6. Grease two baking/cookie sheets. Thinly roll out the mixture on a floured surface and cut out 8cm x 5cm/3in x 2in rectangles, re-rolling the trimmings to make extra pieces. Transfer the shapes to the baking sheets and bake for about 8–10 minutes, until they turn a pale, golden colour around the edges. Allow to stand for a couple of minutes before moving to a wire cooling rack.

2 Put some royal icing in a piping bag fitted with a fine writing tube/tip. Pipe names across the biscuits, keeping

vanilla sable mixture (see page 9)

icing and decoration

double quantity royal icing (see page 9)

edible silver or coloured metallic dusting powder/petal dust/blossom tint

equipment

2 baking/cookie sheets

rolling pin

sharp knife

wire cooling rack

paper piping bag

fine writing tube/tip

greaseproof paper/baking parchment (optional)

fine sieve

makes 28

baking time 8–10 minutes

the letters away from the edges. (You may prefer to practise a few names on a sheet of greaseproof paper/baking parchment first.)

3 Pipe a line of icing around the edges of the name to create an oval-shaped frame. Pipe loops of icing that just meet the first line and form points around the edges of the rectangles.

4 Use more icing to fill in the centres of the loops, generously filling each section. Pipe further curved lines in the gaps around the edges. Leave the place names to set for at least 2 hours.

5 Put a little dusting powder/petal dust/blossom tint in a fine sieve. Holding it about 10cm/4in above the biscuits, lightly sprinkle the dusting powder over the place names. Transfer the shapes to an airtight container and store in a cool place for up to three days.

TIP Once the biscuits are set, they can be stacked in an airtight container. However, do not make the piles any deeper than three biscuits, and weave greaseproof paper between each layer. If you have time, it is better to dust the biscuits (step 5) on the actual day of the celebration. The place names can also be used for other occasions, such as special dinner parties.

Toucans

These cheerful birds will certainly add colour and fun to a special family tea or celebration. Perch them among plant foliage for extra effect.

1 Preheat the oven to 200°C/400°F/Gas Mark 6. Grease two baking/cookie sheets. Trace the toucan template on page 124 on to paper and cut it out. Roll out the mixture on a floured surface and cut out the toucan shapes using the template and a sharp knife.

2 Transfer the toucan shapes to the baking sheets and bake them in the oven for about 12 minutes, until they turn a deep golden colour. Leave the birds on the baking sheets for a couple of minutes, before carefully transferring them to a wire rack to cool.

light gingerbread mixture (see page 8)

icing and decoration

royal icing (see page 9)

blue food colouring

85g/3oz red sugarpaste/rolled fondant

icing/confectioners' sugar for dusting

60g/2oz white sugarpaste

30g/1oz orange sugarpaste

equipment

2 baking/cookie sheets

paper for template (see page 124)

rolling pin

sharp knife

wire cooling rack

paper piping bags

fine writing tube/tip

wooden cocktail stick/toothpick

fine paintbrush

makes 12–14

baking time 12 minutes

Add blue food colouring to the royal icing and transfer about a third of the quantity to a piping bag fitted with a fine writing tube/tip. Thin the remaining blue icing until it has the consistency of thick pouring cream and transfer the mixture into another piping bag.

Thinly roll the red sugarpaste/rolled fondant on a surface dusted with icing/confectioners' sugar. Use the template to cut out beaks and position these on the birds, securing the paste into position with a small amount of the unthinned royal icing. With the tip of the knife, define the upper and lower areas of the beak by marking a slightly curved line across the surface.

Using the unthinned icing, pipe a line from the top of the beak along the outline of the bird. Take the icing up and around the edge of the wing but leave space for the white breast to be positioned. Pipe another line around the edge of the breast to the bottom of the beak. Repeat on all the toucans.

Snip off the tip of the thinned icing bag and use this to flood the icing over the toucans, within the piped lines. The icing should fill the area in a thin, even layer. Use a wooden cocktail stick/toothpick to spread the icing to the edges and corners. Leave the birds aside to set for about an hour.

7 Thinly roll the white sugarpaste and cut out the breasts using the template and knife. Position the breastplates on the birds, securing them with a small amount of royal icing from the bag. Press firmly, to ensure the sugarpaste adheres to the surface.

8 Roll out the orange sugarpaste into a thin layer and cut out the eyes. Press these gently into position on the blue icing, again using some royal icing to hold the sugarpaste in position.

9 Using blue food colouring and a fine paintbrush, paint on the eyes and feather details. Leave the birds aside to set overnight. Store the biscuits in an airtight container for up to three days.

TIPS Once you have used the toucan templates to cut out the biscuit shapes, cut out the beak, breastplate and eye shapes from the template. The small paper pieces can then be used to cut out the sugarpaste shapes more accurately.

Try alternative colour combinations to imitate the colourful plumage of tropical birds. Combinations of bright orange, yellow, blue, green and red are all extremely effective, and will brighten any table arrangement or room.

Giant birthday cookie

Presenting one huge cookie makes the perfect gift for anyone who prefers eating cookies to cakes! Arrange it in a shallow box with candles for extra effect.

1 Preheat the oven to 180°C/350°F/Gas Mark 4. Place the flan ring or loose base cake tin/pan on a baking/cookie sheet and lightly grease. Alternatively, grease the cake tin/pan. Mix together the flour, oats and soda. Melt the butter in a saucepan with the muscovado sugar and syrup. Pour over the flour mixture and mix until evenly combined. Transfer to the flan ring/ tin and spread almost to the edges.

2 Bake for 15–18 minutes until golden. (The mixture will be very soft and wobbly but will firm up on cooling.)

125g/4oz/1 cup self-raising flour
125g/4oz/1⅓ cups porridge oats
½ teaspoon bicarbonate of soda/baking soda
125g/4oz/½ cup unsalted butter
100g/3½oz/generous ½ cup light muscovado sugar
3 tablespoons golden/corn syrup
icing and decoration
100g/3½oz/¾ cup icing/confectioners' sugar
4–5 teaspoons lemon juice
225g/7oz/1½ cups mixed dried fruits e.g. mango, papaya and melon

40g/1¼oz/⅓ cup unblanched almonds, roughly halved
equipment
23cm/9in plain flan ring or loose base cake tin/pan
baking/cookie sheet
wire cooling rack
paper piping bag
makes 1
baking time 15–18 minutes

Loosen the mixture from the edges of the tin and leave for 10 minutes, then transfer to a wire rack to cool.

3 To make the icing, blend the icing/confectioners' sugar with the lemon juice until the mixture thickly coats the back of a spoon. Spoon into a piping bag and snip off the tip so the icing flows in a line about 5mm/¼in thick.

4 Pipe a wavy line of icing around the edges of the cookie to within 1cm/½in of the edges.

5 Mix together the dried fruits and nuts and arrange them over the icing, pressing them down gently.

6 Using more icing from the bag, scribble lines back and forth over the fruit and nuts as decoration. Pipe the recipient's name, or a birthday message, into the centre of the cookie. Leave to set for a couple of hours before packaging or storing. Keep in an airtight container for up to three days.

TIP If you are nervous about piping the name or message on to the cookie, cut out small letters in thin card and lay them on the centre of the surface. Transfer the icing to another paper piping bag and snip off a much smaller tip. Pipe around the letters, then remove them and fill in the centres with more icing.

Ladybirds

Add a splash of colour to a party with a family of ladybirds. If you do not have very small, round cutters to shape the spots, use the ends of piping tubes/tips.

Preheat the oven to 200°C/400°F/Gas Mark 6. Grease two baking/cookie sheets. Trace the ladybird body and head templates on page 124 on to paper and cut out.

Roll out the vanilla sable mixture on a floured surface and cut out the body shapes using the template and a sharp knife. (Keep the template for shaping the red icing.) Re-roll the trimmings and cut out an equal number of heads. Transfer the pieces to the baking sheets. Bake for about 8–10 minutes until they turn golden around the edges. Transfer them to a wire cooling rack.

vanilla sable mixture (see page 9)

icing and decoration

royal icing (see page 9)

200g/7oz red sugarpaste/rolled fondant

icing/confectioners' sugar for dusting

75g/3oz black sugarpaste

equipment

2 baking/cookie sheets

paper for templates (see page 124)

rolling pin

sharp knife or scalpel

wire cooling rack

paper piping bag

medium writing tube/tip

2.5cm/1in and 1.5cm/⅝in round cutters

paintbrush

makes 12

baking time 8–10 minutes

3 Put some royal icing into a paper piping bag fitted with a medium writing tube/tip. Thinly roll the red sugarpaste/rolled fondant on a surface lightly dusted with icing/confectioners' sugar. Use the knife and template to cut out the bodies.

4 Pipe a small amount of icing on to the ladybird shapes and position the red sugarpaste on top. Secure the heads in place with a little more icing.

5 Roll out the black sugarpaste very thinly and cut out plenty of circles using the two small round cutters. Secure in position using a dampened paintbrush. For the dots

right on the edges of the ladybirds, simply position them so they overhang, then cut off the excess paste with a scalpel or knife.

6 Using the icing in the bag, pipe large blobs for the eyes and then the antennae. Roll small balls of black icing and press them into the centres of the eyes, for the pupils. Roll some larger balls for the ends of the antennae and fix into position. Shape and secure each mouth using red icing trimmings.

7 Leave the ladybirds aside for 2 hours before storing them in an airtight container for up to three days.

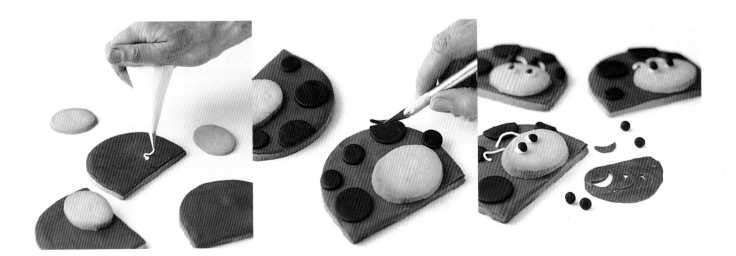

Juggling clowns

These wacky colours and fun features make clowns the perfect characters for children's parties. Prop them up against tumblers and dishes for instant colour.

1 Preheat the oven to 200°C/400°F/Gas Mark 6 and grease two baking/cookie sheets. Trace the template on page 124 on to paper and cut it out.

2 Roll out the light gingerbread mixture on a floured surface and cut out the clown shapes using the template. Transfer the pieces to the baking sheets and bake them for 12–15 minutes until they turn a golden colour around the edges. Leave the pieces on the tray for around 2 minutes to harden slightly, before transferring them to a wire cooling rack.

light gingerbread mixture (see page 8)

icing and decoration

royal icing (see page 9)

icing/confectioners' sugar for dusting

125g/4oz blue sugarpaste/rolled fondant

125g/4oz lilac sugarpaste

85g/3oz orange sugarpaste

60g/2oz red sugarpaste

equipment

2 baking/cookie sheets

paper for template (see page 124)

rolling pin

sharp knife

wire cooling rack

paper piping bags

fine and large writing tubes/tips

fine paintbrush

greaseproof paper/baking parchment

makes 16

baking time 12–15 minutes

3 Put some royal icing in a piping bag fitted with a fine writing tube/tip. Spoon more of the icing into a piping bag fitted with a large writing tube.

4 Lightly dust the work surface with icing/confectioners' sugar. Roll the blue and lilac sugarpaste/rolled fondant under the palms of your hands into two thin sausages. Press the two pieces together and then fold, twist and roll them into each other about three times, so that the colours become lightly marbled.

5 Roll the marbled sugarpaste into a thin layer. Remove the hands, feet and head from the clown template, to leave just the suit, and use this to cut out a suit shape in the icing. Pipe a small amount of icing on to a biscuit and secure the sugarpaste suit in position, smoothing it down gently with your fingers. Repeat this process with the remaining shapes. You may need to re-roll the trimmings in order to get extra suits – this will probably cause the colours to become even more marbled.

6 Thinly roll the orange sugarpaste and use a knife to cut out shapes for the hats and boots. (You can use the template as a guide if necessary.) Secure these pieces of sugarpaste to the clowns using a small amount of royal icing, as before. Shape small buttons out of the

suparpaste and carefully secure these to the clowns' suits with a dampened paintbrush.

7 Roll out the red sugarpaste thinly and cut out shapes for the pockets. Use the dampened paintbrush and icing to secure these to the suits. Roll tiny balls of icing for the noses and curved shapes for the mouths. Secure the pieces with dots of icing from the bag with the fine writing tube. Roll small balls of the blue icing trimmings and secure these at the tops of the hats.

8 Use the piping bag fitted with the large writing tube to pipe the frilly collars. Use the icing bag with the fine tube to add the wrists and ankles. Finish by piping on the eye and mouth details. Leave the clowns aside to set for 2 hours.

9 Store the clowns for up to four days in an airtight container. Be sure to use a shallow container and interleave greaseproof paper/baking parchment between each of the biscuit layers.

TIP In addition to propping the clowns up on the dining table, they can also be used for decorating the party room. Simply tie fine ribbon around their waists and hang them around the room.

Gingerbread spice hearts

These aromatic, spice-studded hearts are particularly easy to make and are ideal for anniversaries, Valentine events or rustic, country-style weddings.

1 Preheat the oven to 200°C/400°F/Gas Mark 6. Grease two baking/cookie sheets. Roll out the dark gingerbread mixture on a floured surface and cut out heart shapes using the large heart-shaped cutter.

2 Using the smaller cutter, cut out the centres from about half the total number of hearts. Press the whole star anise into the centre of the remaining shapes.

3 Transfer all the shapes, including the centres, to the baking sheets. Bake the shapes for about 12 minutes until

dark gingerbread mixture (see page 8)
about 10 whole star anise
icing and decoration
3 tablespoons cardamom pods
85g/3oz crystallized ginger pieces
1 tablespoon lightly beaten egg white
finely grated rind of half an orange
1 tablespoon orange juice
150g/5oz/1¼ cups icing/confectioners' sugar, sifted
3 tablespoons whole cloves

equipment
2 baking/cookie sheets
rolling pin
7.5cm/3in and 2.5cm/1in heart-shaped cutters
wire cooling rack
pestle and mortar
paper piping bag
makes 20
baking time 12 minutes

they have risen slightly. Leave the hearts to stand for a couple of minutes, before transferring them to a wire cooling rack.

4 Using either a pestle and mortar or a small bowl and the end of a rolling pin, lightly crush the cardamom pods to reveal the seeds, then chop the crystallized ginger into very fine pieces.

5 Beat the egg white in a bowl with the orange rind, juice and icing/confectioners' sugar until the mixture is thick enough to just hold its shape. Spoon this into a piping bag and snip off the tip so that the icing flows in a line

about 5mm/¼in thick. Use the icing to pipe thick, wavy lines around the edges of the hearts.

6 Press the cardamom pods, ginger and cloves into the icing. Leave the hearts aside for 2 hours to set before storing them in an airtight container for up to five days.

TIP If you want to hang the hearts, make a hole 1cm/½in away from the top of each with a skewer before baking. (Do not forget to re-shape the holes when the pieces come out of the oven.) Once decorated, thread with fine ribbon – the hearts can be hung around the room for maximum effect.

Autumn leaves

Capture the stunning colours of fallen, autumnal leaves on these eyecatching treats. It is worth spending some time getting a realistic blend of colours.

1 Preheat the oven to 200°C/400°F/Gas Mark 6 and grease two baking/cookie sheets. Trace the autumn leaf templates on page 124 on to a sheet of paper and cut out. Roll out the chocolate sable mixture on a floured surface and cut out the leaf shapes, using the templates and a scalpel. Make about the same number of leaves in each shape.

2 Transfer the pieces to the baking sheets and bake for about 12 minutes, until the mixture rises slightly. After baking, transfer the leaf shapes to a wire cooling rack.

chocolate sable mixture (see page 9)

icing and decoration
icing glaze (see page 9)
orange, yellow and brown food colourings
royal icing (see page 9)

equipment
2 baking/cookie sheets
paper for template (see page 124)
rolling pin
scalpel
wire cooling rack
paper piping bags
large pastry brush

makes 20
baking time 12 minutes

3 Divide the icing glaze evenly among three small cups or bowls. Colour one quantity of the glaze orange, another deep yellow and the third a warm brown. Mix a tablespoonful of each with a third of the royal icing to make a paler shade of each colour. Put these lighter coloured icings in piping bags and keep aside for use later.

4 Using the large pastry brush, spread one of the icing glaze colours over one of the leaf shapes, to form a thin covering. Repeat for the other similarly-shaped leaves. Then do the same using the other two icing glazes on the remaining two leaf shapes.

5 Pipe fine veins on to each of the leaves, with the piping bags and coloured glazes. Use the light orange on the orange leaves, the light yellow on the yellow leaves and so on.

6 Leave the pieces aside to set for 2–3 hours. They can then be stored in an airtight container for up to four days.

TIP Red and yellow food colourings can be mixed together to make orange, but avoid colours that are too bright and garish. Add a little extra brown to tone colours down, or a little red to warm them up.

Halloween tealights

If you are planning a Halloween night buffet or dinner, these decorative lights will certainly add a sense of atmosphere to the proceedings.

1 Preheat the oven to 200°C/400°F/Gas Mark 6. Grease a large baking/cookie sheet. Trace the pumpkin template on page 124 on to paper and cut it out.

2 Roll out the dark gingerbread mixture on a floured surface and cut around the outer edges of the template with a sharp knife. Transfer the pumpkin shape to the baking sheet. Cut out three more pumpkin shapes, making sure you cut a straight line across the base of each so that they will sit squarely on the round bases. Gather up and re-roll the trimmings. Use the round cutter

dark gingerbread mixture (see page 8)

icing and decoration

royal icing (see page 9)

orange food colouring

30g/1oz green sugarpaste/rolled fondant icing/confectioners' sugar for dusting

equipment

large baking/cookie sheet

paper for template (see page 124)

rolling pin

sharp knife or scalpel

7cm/2¾in round cutter

wire cooling rack

paper piping bag

large writing tube/tip

tealights

makes 4

baking time 15 minutes

to cut out out four circles for the biscuit bases from this remaining gingerbread mixture.

3 Lay the pumpkin template back over the shapes. Cut out and remove the marked features using the tip of a small knife or a scalpel. Bake all the shapes for about 15 minutes until slightly risen. Transfer to a wire cooling rack and leave to cool.

4 Colour the royal icing with orange food colouring. Put the icing in a piping bag fitted with a large writing tube/tip. This icing will be used for decorating, and for fixing the sugarpaste/rolled fondant.

5 Thinly roll the green sugarpaste on a surface dusted with icing/confectioners' sugar and cut out some small stalk shapes. (Cut out and use the stalk area of the template as a guide if you prefer.) Pipe a little icing on to the stalk area of the pumpkins and position the stalks, gently pressing down the sugarpaste with your fingers. Mark decorative lines on the stalks with the tip of the knife or scalpel.

6 Use the icing in the bag to pipe an outline around the edges of each pumpkin. Next, outline the holes cut out for the eyes, nose and mouth. Try to keep a steady hand as you work around the outlines.

7 Pipe more lines from the top of the pumpkins down to the base. Curve piped lines towards the outside edges, to accentuate the round shape of the pumpkins.

8 Pipe several thick, straight lines of icing over the round gingerbread bases, about 1cm/½in away from the edges. Gently press the pumpkin pieces into the icing. Pipe another line of icing along the back of the pumpkin where it joins the base – this will help to provide additional support. Prop the pumpkins up with tumblers or small glasses until the icing has set. Leave aside for at least 2 hours, or preferably overnight, to set completely, before storing in an airtight container or tin.

TIPS The pumpkins make attractive decorations for dining tables, shelves or mantlepieces. Positioning small tealights around the base will help to set them off, and adds to the Halloween atmosphere, although beware that the heat will eventually soften the icing. For a more traditional occasion or children's party, you could always change the facial expressions and replace the smiling mouth with sharp, irregular teeth!

If you do not have any suitable containers that are large enough to store the pumpkin shapes, put them on a tray or board and cover them loosely with cling film/plastic wrap. This will help to create an airtight seal.

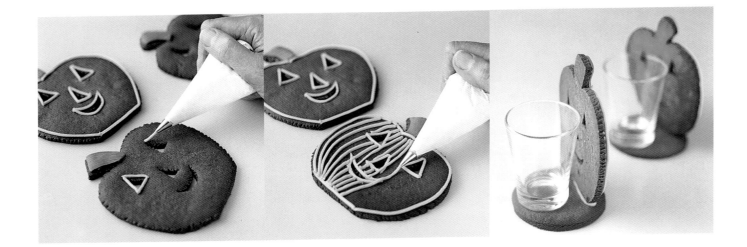

Christmas

Gingerbread cottage

Often associated with the characters Hansel and Gretel, this gingerbread house makes a good cake alternative for a winter birthday or Christmas party.

1 Preheat the oven to 200°C/400°F/Gas Mark 6 and grease two baking/cookie sheets. Trace the templates on page 125 on to sheets of paper and cut out. Thinly roll out the dark gingerbread mixture and cut out the cottage shapes. The front of the cottage requires a door to be cut, so use the template to cut out the door and then trim 5mm/¼in off the base of the door. Cut out a window from the area above the door using the round cutter.

2 Transfer all the pieces to the baking sheets, including the door, and bake for about 15 minutes until slightly risen.

dark gingerbread mixture (see page 8)

icing and decoration

royal icing (see page 9)

10 small ratafia biscuits/cookies

85g/3oz chocolate-covered raisins

about 15–18 chocolates or small truffles

small packet candy-covered chocolates

7 small wafer-thin chocolate biscuits/cookies

1 small chocolate-covered fudge bar, thinly sliced

equipment

2 baking/cookie sheets

paper for templates (see page 125)

rolling pin and sharp knife

4cm/1½in round cutter

wire cooling rack

paper piping bag

board or rectangular plate, about 28cm x 20cm/11in x 8in

palette knife/metal spatula

makes 1 cottage

baking time 15 minutes

Leave the pieces on the tray for 2 minutes, before transferring them to a wire cooling rack.

3 Spread a little icing along the base and up the sides of one side section. Spread more icing along the base of the front section and secure the two sections together on the board, propping up the biscuits with small glasses or tumblers for support until they have set. Secure the back section, then the other side, and leave for about 30 minutes to set slightly.

4 Spread more icing over the top edges of the side pieces and secure one of the roof sections, again using glasses or tumblers to give the shapes support. Spread a little icing along the top of the roof and secure the other piece in place.

5 Using a palette knife/metal spatula, spread a thin layer of icing over the roof. If the icing feels stiff and will not spread easily, thin it with a little water.

6 For the icicles, hold a teaspoon of icing at an angle above the edges of the roof. As the icing starts to slip from the spoon, catch it along the edges, to create the impression of dangling icicles. (Again, if the icing is too stiff, thin it with a little water first.)

7 Use the ratafia biscuits/cookies, chocolates and chocolate-covered raisins to decorate the roof. The pieces can be positioned randomly, but add a single row of chocolate raisins along the top of the roof for the top tiles.

8 Spoon a little more icing into the piping bag and put this aside for later use. Then spread the remaining icing over the board.

9 Pipe a little icing on to the backs of the chocolate biscuits and secure them on either side of the window. Arrange the remaining biscuits at the front of the cottage, to create the impression of doorsteps.

10 Pipe a line of icing around the door arch and press the door in position. Decorate the window ledges and round window with chocolate-covered raisins, securing each into position with a dab of icing. Secure another raisin for the doorknob and place a few candy covered disks on the iced-board to suggest a path.

11 Use the icing in the bag to pipe decorative edges around the door and along the corners of the cottage. Add small chocolate fudge slices around the base.

TIP Before positioning the roof, you could fill the house with chocolate and sweet treats for an extra surprise.

Stained glass candles

In this recipe, crushed boiled sweets are baked in gingerbread 'frames'. The idea is that they melt and then set brittle as they cool, to create glass-like panels.

dark gingerbread mixture (see page 8)

icing and decoration

250g/8oz clear boiled fruit sweets/candies, in a mixture of colours

royal icing (see page 9)

red or orange food colouring

4 nightlights

equipment

2 baking/cookie sheets

bakewell/non-stick paper

3cm/1¼in square cutter or small sharp knife

rolling pin

wooden cocktail sticks/toothpicks

paper piping bag

medium writing tube/tip

makes 4 lights

baking time 10 minutes

1 Preheat the oven to 200°C/400°F/Gas Mark 6. Line two baking/cookie sheets with bakewell/non-stick paper. Thinly roll out the dark gingerbread mixture on a floured surface and cut out twelve 12cm x 8cm/4¾in x 3in rectangles. (You will probably need to cut out the squares from some of the biscuits and then re-roll the trimmings to make sufficient quantities.) Transfer the rectangles to the lined baking sheets, spacing them slightly apart.

2 Use a square cutter to cut out six squares from each piece, leaving a fine windowpane-effect frame.

Alternatively, you could use the tip of a knife to cut out the squares. Any of the internal squares that you haven't needed to re-roll can be baked separately to avoid wastage. Bake the pieces for 5 minutes, then remove the baking sheets from the oven and leave aside to cool.

3 Very lightly crush the sweets/candies, while still in their wrappers, by tapping them with a rolling pin. (If the sweets are not individually wrapped, put them in a polythene bag before crushing them.) Unseal the wrappers/bag and place a few pieces of crushed sweet in each square of the frames. (You will need about three sweets to fill each rectangle.)

4 Return the baking sheet to the oven for a further 5 minutes until the sweets have melted. If there are any squares that are not completely flooded with the melted sweet, use wooden cocktail sticks/toothpicks to ease the mixture up to the edges. (You will need to do this as soon as the biscuits are removed from the oven, because the sweets will harden and become brittle very quickly.) Leave the pieces on the baking sheets to cool completely.

5 Brightly colour the royal icing with red or orange food colouring and spoon it into a piping bag fitted with a medium writing tube/tip. Pipe decorative lines over the gingerbread. Leave this to set for about 30 minutes.

6 Carefully peel the paper away from the panels. Pipe a little icing down the edges of three of the biscuits and secure them together in a triangle. If necessary, use a few small glasses to prop up the frames until they are set. Repeat with the remaining biscuits and leave for about 2 hours or overnight to set.

7 To display, light each nightlight and then lower the frame over the light. The decorations should last at least a full evening without melting – possibly even two or three!

TIPS When removing the biscuits from the paper lined sheets, carefully peel the paper away from the shapes.

This is better than lifting the biscuits away from the paper, as the biscuit pieces are liable to crack.

Once exposed to the atmosphere, the melted sweets will gradually begin to soften, so if you want to make them in advance, leave them on their baking sheets and cover tightly with cling film/plastic wrap for up to three days. For convenience, you can assemble them up to 24 hours before they are required.

To protect the dining table from melted wax, cut triangles of thick card to fit to the base of the nightlights. You can then place them under the decorations and candles.

Lace snowflakes

You will be tempted to keep these stars, with their attractive piped snowflake centres, hanging on the Christmas tree throughout the festive season.

1 Preheat the oven to 200°C/400°F/Gas Mark 6. Lightly grease two baking/cookie sheets. Roll out the vanilla sable mixture on a floured surface and cut out star shapes using the large star cutter. Transfer the star shapes to the baking sheets.

2 Using the small star cutter, cut out the centre of each star. If the cutter starts to stick to the dough, clean it and dust with a little flour. Re-roll the trimmings as necessary to make 14 star biscuits in total. Bake for 6–7 minutes until they turn golden around the edges. Leave

vanilla sable mixture (see page 9)

icing and decoration
icing glaze (see page 9)
edible white glitter
royal icing (see page 9)
fine white or silver ribbon

equipment
2 baking/cookie sheets
11cm/4½in and 6cm/2½in
large and small 6-point star cutters
wire cooling rack

greaseproof paper/baking parchment
pastry brush
fine paintbrush
bakewell/non-stick paper
paper piping bag
medium writing tube/tip
makes 14
baking time 7 minutes

the biscuits on the baking sheet for 2 minutes, then carefully transfer them to a wire cooling rack.

3 Place a tray or sheet of greaseproof paper/baking parchment under the rack. (Use two racks or ice biscuits in two batches as they will not all fit on one rack.) Using a pastry brush, coat the top side of the stars with icing glaze. Brush any icing away from the inner points with a fine paintbrush. Leave for about 1 hour until touch dry.

4 Brush the stars very lightly with a clean, dampened pastry brush and sprinkle with edible glitter. Do not make the biscuits wet because the icing may dissolve.

5 Lift the biscuits off the rack and lay them on a sheet of bakewell/non-stick paper. Shave off any drips of icing from the undersides of the stars if they are not sitting flat on the paper. Put some royal icing in a piping bag fitted with a medium writing tube/tip.

6 Pipe three lines across each star from the inner points of the star so that they cross in the centre. Pipe little snowflake designs over the crossed lines as decoration. Leave overnight to set.

7 Carefully peel the paper away and use lengths of ribbon to hang the snowflakes from the tree.

Gift tag trees

These Christmas tree-shaped gift tags really add a personal touch to presents. Thread them with ribbon or string to match the wrapping paper.

1 Preheat the oven to 200°C/400°F/Gas Mark 6. Trace the tree template on page 126 on to a sheet of paper and cut out. Grease two baking/cookie sheets.

2 Roll out the vanilla sable mixture on a floured surface. Use the template and knife to cut out the tree shapes. Re-roll the trimmings if necessary to make 14–16 tree shapes. Transfer to the baking sheets.

3 Using a skewer, make a small hole near the top of each tree, about 1cm/¹⁄₂in away from the edges, ready for

vanilla sable mixture (see page 9)
100g/3¹⁄₂oz/1 cup flaked/slivered almonds
icing and decoration
royal icing (see page 9)
dragees
equipment
paper for template (see page 126)
baking/cookie sheet
rolling pin
sharp knife
metal skewer

wire cooling rack
paper piping bag
medium writing tube/tip
fine ribbon or string
makes 14–16
baking time 8 minutes

threading the ribbon or string. Make sure each hole measures at least 2mm/^{1}/₁₆in across or you may have difficulty threading the ribbon through them.

4 Pick out the perfectly-shaped flaked/slivered almonds and lightly toast them under a high grill/broiler. To decorate the gift tags, arrange the almonds in rows across the dough and press the tops in slightly.

5 Bake for about 8 minutes until golden around the edges. Immediately re-mark the holes as they may have shrunk during baking. Leave on the baking sheets for 2 minutes, then transfer to a wire cooling rack.

6 Put the icing in a piping bag fitted with a medium writing tube/tip. Pipe wavy lines over the almonds on the biscuits. Press silver balls/dragees into the icing at intervals. Leave to set for about an hour, then transfer to an airtight container.

7 Thread the gift tags with ribbon or string and secure to the wrapped presents.

TIPS To avoid breakages, secure the gift tags to fairly large parcels, to ensure they are well supported.

You will not need all the flaked almonds – this quantity enables you to pick the best shapes out to use.

Christmas baubles

For a really effective Christmas display, thread these baubles on long ribbons and hang them over the mantlepiece or on the Christmas tree.

1 Preheat the oven to 200°C/400°F/Gas Mark 6. Grease two baking/cookie sheets. Roll out the light gingerbread mixture on a floured surface and use the two cutters to cut out circles. Transfer these to the baking sheets. Using the skewer, make a small hole through the dough about 1cm/½in away from the edge of each biscuit.

2 Bake the biscuits for 10–12 minutes, until they turn golden around the edges. Immediately re-mark the holes in the biscuits because they may have shrunk during baking. Transfer the biscuits to a wire cooling rack.

light gingerbread mixture (see page 8)

icing and decoration
triple quantity of royal icing (see page 9)
blue, green and red food colourings
fine blue, red or green ribbon

equipment
2 baking/cookie sheets
rolling pin
9cm/3½in and 7.5cm/3in round cutters
metal skewer
wire cooling rack

paper for templates (see page 125)
paper piping bags
medium writing tube/tip
cling film/plastic wrap
greaseproof paper/baking parchment
medium paintbrush
makes 12 large and 12 small baubles
baking time 10–12 minutes

3 Trace the bauble templates (see page 125) on to a sheet of paper and cut them out. Spoon a quarter of the royal icing into a piping bag fitted with the medium writing tube/tip. Divide the remaining icing between three small bowls. Add blue colouring to one, green to the second and red to the third. Thin each batch with a few drops of water until the icing has the consistency of thick pouring cream. Cover the surfaces with cling film/plastic wrap to prevent a crust forming.

4 Arrange the biscuits in a single layer on the wire cooling rack and place a tray or sheet of greaseproof paper/baking parchment underneath. Position the large

bauble template on one large biscuit and pipe a line of royal icing on to the biscuit, around the curved edges of the paper. Use the same technique on all the biscuits, using the smaller template on the small biscuits. Pipe a circle of icing around the skewered holes.

5 Place the red icing in a piping bag and snip off the tip. Use this to 'flood' the top and bottom area of each bauble. Ease the icing over the sides with a fine paintbrush in order to completely coat the biscuit. Leave to dry.

6 Place the blue icing in a piping bag. Snip off the tip and flood the central areas of each of the biscuits. If

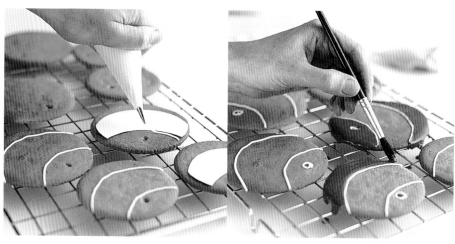

necessary, use a paintbrush to take the blue right up to the white iced lines. Leave the biscuits overnight to dry and set.

7 Pipe little triangular tree shapes on to half the biscuits with white icing, and pipe a star at the tip of some of the trees. Pipe dots of white icing on the blue area around the trees. Pipe white, holly-shaped outlines on to the remaining baubles, with little circles for berries.

8 Put the green icing into a piping bag, snip off the tip and use this to fill the tree and holly shapes. Ease the icing into the corners of the shapes with a paintbrush.

Fill the berry outlines with dots of red icing. Leave overnight to set.

9 Use more white icing to pipe over the initial template lines. Finally, thread the baubles with lengths of fine ribbon for hanging from trees or parcels.

TIP These biscuits appear to take a long time to decorate because they need to be left overnight twice. This is to ensure that the colours do not run and to prevent the white from losing its vibrancy. However, the finished results are well worth the effort, making decorative baubles that outshine any commercial varieties.

Festive table centre

This spectacular decoration makes a wonderful table centrepiece throughout the festive season. Pick the biscuits from the tree as you enjoy after-dinner coffee.

light gingerbread mixture (see page 8)

icing and decoration

double quantity royal icing (see page 9)

hazelnuts in their shells

dried apricots, prunes or glacé fruits

silver/coloured sugar almonds

icing/confectioners' sugar for dusting

equipment

baking/cookie sheet

cardboard tube

aluminium foil

1 Preheat the oven to 200°C/400°F/Gas Mark 6. Lightly grease a baking/cookie sheet. Wrap the cardboard tube, which can be taken from an empty roll of foil or kitchen paper, in aluminium foil. Put more foil in the Swiss/jelly roll tin, so that it loosely lines the edges, and lay the tube on top. Lightly grease the foil.

2 Roll out half the light gingerbread mixture on to a floured surface. Using a sharp knife, cut out some simple leaf shapes, about 5cm/2in long and 2.5cm/1in at the widest point. Carefully mark a vein line down the

swiss/jelly roll tin

rolling pin

sharp knife

5cm/2in star cutter

wire cooling rack

metal or cane topiary cone, about 28cm/11in high and 20cm/8in across base

28cm/11in board or plate

palette knife/metal spatula

makes 1 gingerbread tree

baking time 8 minutes

centre of the leaves with the knife, and transfer them to the greased baking sheet.

3 Roll out the remaining mixture and use the knife to cut out out two small star shapes. (One star will serve as a spare in case of breakages.) Place the stars on the baking sheet.

4 Cut out further leaves from the remaining dough, and arrange some of these leaves along the foil cylinder, so that they will bake in a slightly curved shape. Lay the remaining biscuit shapes around the edges of the foil-lined tin.

5 Bake all the shapes for 6–8 minutes until they turn golden. Transfer the flat leaves to a wire cooling rack.

6 Wrap the topiary cone tightly in foil, tucking the ends underneath, and position on the plate. Use a palette knife/metal spatula to spread a thick layer of royal icing over the surface of the foil.

7 Starting at the top, press the hazelnuts into the icing. Gradually work down and around the frame, creating a spiral helter-skelter effect. Then press a row of dried apricots into the icing, next to the nuts. Alternatively, use prunes or glacé fruit.

8 Following the same pattern, press a row of silver-coloured sugar almonds into the icing. Space the almonds equally between the nuts and apricots, as you work down and around the cone.

9 Use the biscuits to fill the uncovered areas of the cone, overlapping them slightly at the tips. If they do not adhere immediately, apply additional royal icing to the frame and/or base of the biscuit.

10 Secure the star to the top of the cone with a little more icing. Leave to set for at least 2 hours. Serve dusted generously with icing/confectioners' sugar.

TIPS Do not make this decoration too far in advance if you are planning to serve it after dinner with coffee. This is because the biscuits will gradually soften when exposed to the atmosphere. If you prefer, make the centrepiece up to three days in advance and wrap it loosely in cling film/plastic wrap to make an airtight seal and prevent the biscuits from drying out.

A range of edible decorations can be used instead of the hazelnuts, sugared almonds and dried apricots. For example, shelled walnuts, pecans, brazil nuts, prunes, dates and chunks of crystallized ginger all look equally effective spiralling down the cone.

Festive skyscapes

These colourful, Middle Eastern style biscuits can be displayed on shelves, the dining table or even as hanging decorations on the Christmas tree.

1 Preheat the oven to 200°C/400°F/Gas Mark 6 and grease a large baking/cookie sheet. Trace the two templates on page 125 on to a sheet of paper and cut out the shapes. Roll out the dark gingerbread mixture and use the large template and a sharp knife to cut out ten shapes. If you plan to hang the decorations by ribbon, use a skewer to pierce holes through the top of the pieces, about 1cm/½in from the edge. (These holes will need to be re-marked after baking, as they are likely to close up slightly during baking.) Transfer the pieces to the baking sheet and bake for about 10 minutes until the

dark gingerbread mixture (see page 8)

icing and decoration

royal icing (see page 9)

blue and gold food colourings

200g/7oz red sugarpaste/rolled fondant

icing/confectioners' sugar for dusting

gold and blue dragees

fine ribbon (optional)

equipment

baking/cookie sheet

paper for templates (see page 125)

rolling pin

sharp knife

metal skewer (optional)

wire cooling rack

paper piping bags

medium and fine writing tubes/tips

fine paintbrush

makes 10

baking time 10 minutes

dough has slightly risen. Leave the pieces on the baking sheet for 2 minutes before transferring them to a wire cooling rack.

2 Add blue colouring to half the amount of royal icing. Put the mixture in a paper piping bag fitted with a medium writing tube/tip. Spoon the remaining white icing into a piping bag fitted with a fine writing tube.

3 Thinly roll out the red sugarpaste/rolled fondant on a surface lightly dusted with icing/confectioners' sugar. Use the smaller template and the knife to cut out the shapes of the buildings.

4 Scribble a little white icing across the base of one biscuit and carefully lay the red sugarpaste buildings in position. Repeat this procedure for all the remaining biscuits, each time gently smoothing the sugarpaste down with your fingers to eliminate any bumps.

5 Pipe a fine line of white icing around the edges of the buildings – pipe vertical lines across the red sugarpaste to separate each of the buildings. Also pipe decorative door outlines and windows in various sizes.

6 Use a small amount of icing to secure gold dragees on the roof tops and edges of some of the buildings. Use

more white icing to pipe plenty of stars in the sky above. Among the smaller 'spot stars', pipe one or two larger star shapes.

Pipe icing from the blue icing bag into the centres of the doors and around the edges of the skyscapes. Using a fine paintbrush, paint the roof and window details in gold colouring.

Put the biscuits aside to dry. If you plan to hang the skyscapes as decorations, carefully thread fine ribbon through the holes. The pieces can be tied around the room and hung from window frames and mantelpieces.

TIPS These biscuits also make attractive place setting decorations for a Christmas celebration, in which case you might like to choose icing colours that match your own colour theme. Alternatively, you could display a complete row along a shelf or mantelpiece. To make an upright row, secure several pieces together with icing and prop them up with small glasses or tumblers until they have set.

Gold dusting powder/petal dust can be used instead of gold food colouring, if you prefer. Mix it with a dash of clear spirit, such as vodka, to produce a liquid, paint-like consistency.

Decorated camels

These colourful camels, with their ornate reins, saddles and feet, will be much admired during the festive season. Use a range of colours to brighten the room.

1 Preheat the oven to 200°C/400°F/Gas Mark 6 and grease the two baking/cookie sheets. Trace the camel template on page 126 on to paper and cut out. Roll out the vanilla sable mixture on a floured surface and cut out the camel shapes using the template (see overleaf). Put the template aside for use later on.

2 Carefully transfer the dough pieces to the baking sheets making sure the legs remain straight. Bake for 6–7 minutes or until the edges turn golden. Leave aside for 2 minutes before transferring to a wire cooling rack.

vanilla sable mixture (see page 9)

icing and decoration

royal icing (see page 9)

orange food colouring

60g/2oz purple sugarpaste/rolled fondant

icing/confectioners' sugar for dusting

coloured dragees

small sweets/candies or coloured

cake-decorating baubles

equipment

2 baking/cookie sheets

paper for template (see page 126)

rolling pin

sharp knife

wire cooling rack

paper piping bags

2 fine writing tubes/tips

cling film/plastic wrap

makes 20

baking time 6–7 minutes

3 Colour half the royal icing orange and put it in a piping bag fitted with a fine writing tube/tip. (If necessary, soften the icing with a few drops of water, as stiff icing can be difficult to pipe through fine tubes.) Put some white icing in another piping bag fitted with the other fine writing tube.

4 Thinly roll the purple sugarpaste/rolled fondant on a surface dusted with icing/confectioners' sugar. Cut out the blanket section of the template and use this to cut shapes out of the sugarpaste. Pipe a small amount of icing over the hump of each of the camels and secure the red sugarpaste, smoothing it in place with your fingers.

5 Roll out the purple sugarpaste very thinly and use the knife to cut it into extremely thin strips. Secure the pieces to the camels with a little icing, to create the impression of reins hanging around the animals' heads and necks. Trim off the excess sugarpaste around the edges. It is best to work on a couple of biscuits at a time, in order to prevent the icing strips from drying out before they can be put in position. (Keep the rolled icing covered with a sheet of cling film/plastic wrap, which will help it to remain soft and pliable while you aren't using it.)

6 Press a dragee into each of the reins and decorate them with tiny dots of orange icing.

7 Use the white icing in the second bag to pipe a criss-cross decoration on to the blankets. Then use the orange icing to pipe tassels hanging down from the blankets. Secure dragees into the icing, while it is still soft.

8 Pipe lines of icing around the feet and secure small sweets/candies or baubles. Then pipe the eyes with a little orange icing. Leave the camels aside to dry for 2 hours, then store them in an airtight container for up to three days.

TIPS Although the camels look attractive arranged randomly around the table, they are more effective displayed in an upright position. Try propping them up against candlesticks or vases, or perhaps arrange them in a train along a shelf or dresser. For extra effect, you could create sand dunes using mounds of demerara/brown sugar on a tray or board. Then, arrange the camels in a line along the surface, propping them up with wooden cocktail sticks/toothpicks.

The theme can also be expanded upon. A range of other animals, including horses or elephants, can in fact be made using a freehand or copied template. Indeed, any animal that is traditionally ornamented for festivities could be used to make stunning decorations for all kinds of events, not just Christmas.

Gingerbread nativity scene

This familiar stable scene is made entirely of gingerbread. Gold food colouring adds the finishing touches to this delightful nativity.

light gingerbread mixture (see page 8)

icing and decoration

1 tablespoon lightly beaten egg white

2 tablespoons cocoa powder

brown and gold food colourings

royal icing (see page 9)

75g/2½oz/½ cup demerara/brown sugar

equipment

2 baking/cookie sheets

paper for templates (see page 126)

rolling pin

sharp knife

fine and medium paintbrushes

wire cooling rack

paper piping bags

33cm/13in round or square flat plate

or gold cake board

medium writing tube/tip

thin paintbrush

makes 1 nativity scene

baking time 9–12 minutes

1 Preheat the oven to 200°C/400°F/Gas Mark 6. Grease the two baking/cookie sheets. Trace the nativity templates (see page 126) on to paper and cut out. Roll out the gingerbread mixture on a floured surface and use the templates and a sharp knife to cut out the stable shapes and characters. Transfer the biscuits to a baking sheet.

2 Re-roll the remaining trimmings of gingerbread mixture. Cut out seven rectangles, measuring 5cm x 1cm/2in x ½in, and three rectangles measuring 2cm x 1cm/¾ x ½in, which will become the supports for the characters.

Bake the pieces for about 7–10 minutes until they are just turning golden around the edges. Swap the baking sheets around halfway through cooking.

While the biscuits are baking, mix the egg white with cocoa powder to make a smooth paste. Brush the cocoa paste over the biscuits in the areas shown on the templates, then return all the biscuits to the oven for a further 2 minutes. Carefully transfer the shapes to a wire cooling rack.

Blend a small amount of brown food colouring into about a third of the royal icing. Put the mixture in a piping bag and snip off the tip. Pipe a small amount around the back and sides of the large stable section. Assemble the stable towards the back of the board, carefully securing the two side sections to the back piece. Use small glasses or tumblers to support the sections while they set.

Pipe more icing along the top edges of the stable and on the meeting edges of the roof sections. Carefully secure the roof pieces into place.

Place some white icing in a piping bag fitted with the writing tube/tip. Use this to pipe the details on to all the characters. The shepherds have a simple outline and

headband, while the kings require crowns and robes. Use quick simple swirls for the coats of the sheep and remember to pipe around the edges of the star.

Thin the remaining white icing with a little egg white or water until it has the consistency of thick cream. Put the mixture in a piping bag and snip off the tip. Use this to flood the areas shown on the figures, such as the trim of the kings' robes. Leave to set overnight.

Paint gold food colouring over the piping on the star and kings with a thin paintbrush. Then lightly dust the top of the stable with cocoa powder. Next, spread a little icing along two adjacent sides of the biscuit rectangles. Place these iced sides against the board and the figures, so that the rectangles prop up the biscuits in a vertical position. (Use the longer rectangles for the tall figures and the smaller ones for the shorter figures.) Scatter demerara/brown sugar all around the biscuits to finish.

The gingerbread for the nativity can be baked and stored in an airtight container up to two days before assembling.

A few days after assembly, the biscuits will start to soften, particularly if the scene is positioned in a warm place.

Templates

(All templates should be enlarged by 200%)

Autumn leaves
pp81–83

Juggling clown
pp74–77

Easter chicks
pp32–33

Toucan
pp64–67

Body

Ladybird
pp71–73

Head

Halloween tealights
pp84–87

Seashore shapes
pp54–57

(All templates should be enlarged by 200%)

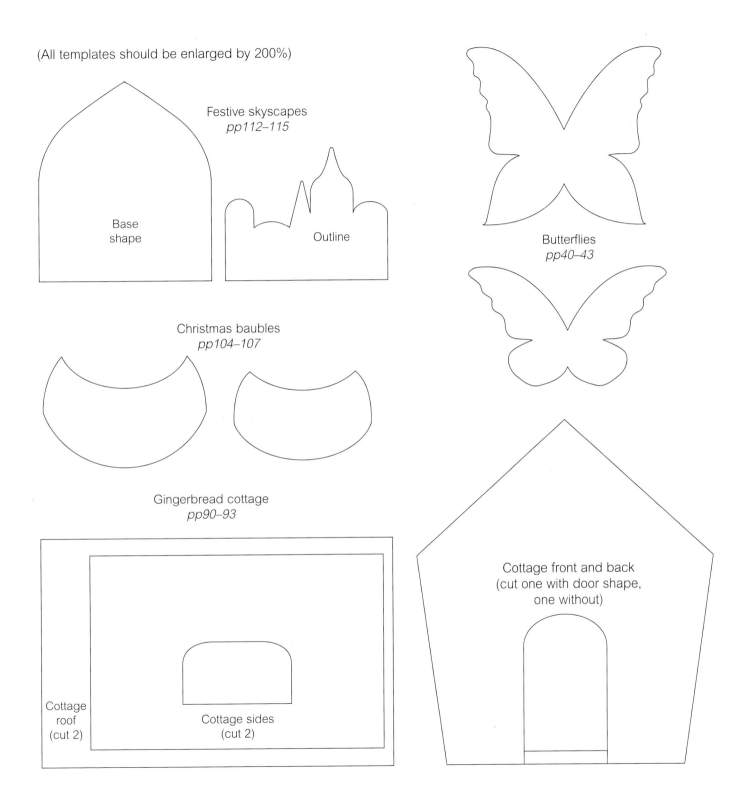

Festive skyscapes
pp112–115

Base
shape

Outline

Butterflies
pp40–43

Christmas baubles
pp104–107

Gingerbread cottage
pp90–93

Cottage front and back
(cut one with door shape,
one without)

Cottage
roof
(cut 2)

Cottage sides
(cut 2)

(All templates should be enlarged by 200%)

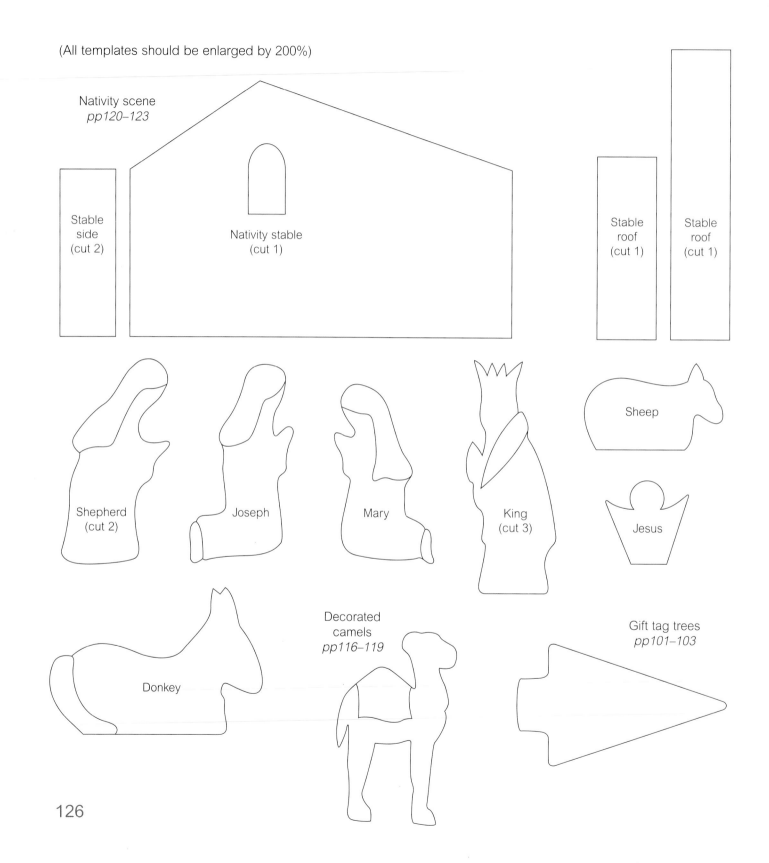

Nativity scene
pp120–123

Stable
side
(cut 2)

Nativity stable
(cut 1)

Stable
roof
(cut 1)

Stable
roof
(cut 1)

Shepherd
(cut 2)

Joseph

Mary

King
(cut 3)

Sheep

Jesus

Donkey

Decorated
camels
pp116–119

Gift tag trees
pp101–103

Index

First published in 2000 by Merehurst Limited
Merehurst is a Murdoch Books (UK) imprint
Copyright © 2000 Merehurst Limited
Photographs © Merehurst Limited
ISBN 1 85391 809 1

Commissioning Editor: Barbara Croxford
Design & Art Direction: Fay Singer
Project Editor: Angela Newton
Photographer: Craig Robertson
Stylist: Penny Markham
CEO: Robert Oerton
Publisher: Catie Ziller
Publishing Manager: Fia Fornari
Production Manager: Lucy Byrne
Group General Manager: Mark Smith
Group CEO/Publisher: Anne Wilson
Colour separation by Colourscan, Singapore
Printed in Singapore by Tien Wah Press

Murdoch Books (UK) Ltd
Ferry House, 51–57 Lacy Road,
Putney, London, SW15 1PR
Tel: +44 (0)20 8355 1480
Fax: +44 (0)20 8355 1499
Murdoch Books (UK) Ltd is a subsidiary
of Murdoch Magazines Pty Ltd.

Murdoch Books®
GPO Box 1203, Sydney,
NSW 1045, Australia
Tel: +61 (0)2 9692 2347
Fax: +61 (0)2 9692 2559
Murdoch Books® is a trademark of
Murdoch Magazines Pty Ltd.